WOLFGANG AMADEUS MOZART

CONCERTO

for Horn and Orchestra
E♭ major/Es-Dur/Mi♭ majeur
K 495

T0081272

Ernst Eulenburg Ltd

London · Mainz · Madrid · New York · Paris · Prague · Tokyo · Toronto · Zürich

Mozart, Horn Concerto in E flat, K.V. 495

Between 1780 and 1790, Mozart wrote four Horn Concertos: the first (K.V.412, a fragment) in D, the other three (K.V.417, 447 and 495) all in E flat. K.V.495 was composed in Vienna on 26th June, 1786, two months after the completion of " Figaro ". Mozart called it "A Horn Concerto for Leitgeb ". Ignaz Leutgeb (or Leitgeb), a conscientious but not brilliant soloist, was formerly a horn player in the Salzburg Orchestra. For him Mozart had written the other concertos, the Concert Rondo K.V.371 and the Quintet K.V.407, and had always taken a delight in teasing him with all sorts of boisterous remarks and challenges. Since 1777 Leutgeb lived in Vienna where he dealt in cheese. Apart from that he still made frequent appearances on the concert platform (Abert, p.50).

The orchestral accompaniment consists of the usual strings, 2 oboes and 2 horns. Köchel (Einstein) remarks about the autograph: " Leipzig, collection Henri Hinrichsen.* Fragments; written, for the fun of it, in blue, red, green, black ink colourfully mixed up. These fragments consist of sheets 13, 14, 21 and 22 (from the collection of Jul. André), sheet 15 (transferred to the possession of C. A. André from the collection Aloys Fuchs) and sheet 23 (in the possession of the Preussische Staatsbibliothek, Berlin), according to Mozart's own numbering. All these sheets then came into the possession of E. Rudorff in Berlin (+31st December, 1916)." With reference to the ending of the Andante and several other places Rudorff (in his report on the revision for the complete edition of Mozart's works) comments on the relations between the autograph sheets and the parts of the first printed edition (pub-

* Now in American private ownership.

Mozart, Hornkonzert Es-dur K.V. 495

Mozart hat vier Hornkonzerte geschrieben, das erste (K.V.412, Fragment) in D-dur, die drei übrigen (K.V.417. 447 und 495) in Es-dur, alle in den 80er Jahren des 18. Jahrhunderts. Das unsrige wurde am 26. Juni 1786, kurz nach dem " Figaro ", in Wien komponiert. " Ein Waldhornkonzert für den Leitgeb ", bezeichnet es Mozart, für denselben früheren Hornisten der Salzburger Kapelle, Ignaz Leutgeb (Leitgeb)—einen tüchtigen, aber nicht höher gebildeten Solobläser—, für den Mozart auch die andern Konzerte, das Konzert-Rondo K.V.371 und das Quintett K.V.407 geschrieben hat und den er gerne mit allen möglichen nicht gerade zarten Bemerkungen und übermütigen Zumutungen zu necken pflegte. Leutgeb wohnte seit 1777 in Wien, führte einen Käsehandel und trat daneben noch häufig in Konzerten auf (Abert S.50). Die Orchesterbegleitung besteht aus den üblichen Streichern, 2 Oboen und 2 Hörnern. Vom Autograph bemerkt Köchel-Einstein: " Leipzig, Sammlung Henri Hinrichsen.* Bruchstücke, Scherzes hal, ber bunt durcheinander in blauerroter, grüner, schwarzer Tinte geschrieben, nach Mozarts Foliierung Blatt 13, 14, 21 und 22 (aus dem Besitz Jul. Andrés), Blatt 15 (aus der Sammlung Aloys Fuchs in C.A. Andrés Besitz übergegangen) und Blatt 23 (der Preuss. Staatsbibliothek Berlin gehörig). Diese sämtlichen Blätter sind dann in den Besitz von E. Rudorff in Berlin (+31. Dezember 1916) gelangt." Im Revisionsbericht zur Mozart-Gesamtausgabe macht Rudorff zum Andanteschluss und zu anderen Stellen Bemerkungen über Verhältnis zwischen den autographen Blättern und der Erstausgabe der Stimmen. Diese letz-

* Jetzt in Amerikanischem Privatbesitz.

lished by André in Offenbach in 1802 as " oeuvre 106 ").

Literature: O. Jahn, Mozart, 1st Edn. III.—Abert-Jahn II.—Wyzewa-St. Foix IV.—Regarding Leitgeb and the Horn Concertos, cf. foreword to K.V.447 (Edition Eulenburg).—Einstein (" Mozart " p.380) points out the relationship with the 1st subject of the first movement of the Cantata " Die Maurerfreude " (K.V.471).

Like the other Horn Concertos, K.V.495 is fresh and lively and admirably adapted to the nature of the solo instrument. Side by side with the concertante element stands true Mozartean melody. As in K.V.447 the 2nd movement is a " Romance ", and the work concludes with a sprightly Rondo in 6/8, a real " hunt "-finale, in which " the true character of the hunting-instrument appears quite unashamedly " (Jahn).

Wilhelm Merian

tere erschien 1802 als " oeuvre 106 " bei André in Offenbach.

Literatur: O. Jahn, Mozart, 1. Aufl. III.—Abert-Jahn II.—Wyzewa-St. Foix IV.-Ueber Leitgeb und die Hornkonzerte siehe auch Vorwort zu K.V.447 in der Edition Eulenburg.—Einstein (" Mozart " S.380) weist auf die Beziehung des 1. Themas im ersten Satz zur Kantate " Die Maurerfreude " (K.V.471) hin.

Auch dieses Konzert ist ein Stück von natürlicher Frische und dem Soloinstrument auf den Leib geschrieben. Neben Konzertantem steht echt Mozartische Gesanglichkeit. Wie bei K.V.447 ist der 2. Satz eine " Romanze ", und das Ganze schliesst wie alle andern Hornkonzerte mit einem frischen Sechsachteltakt-Rondo, einem richtigen " Jagd " finale, in dem " die ursprüngliche Natur des Jagdinstruments ganz unverhohlen zum Vorschein kommt " (Jahn).

Wilhelm Merian

CONCERTO

I.

W. A. Mozart
1756-1791
Köchel N? 495

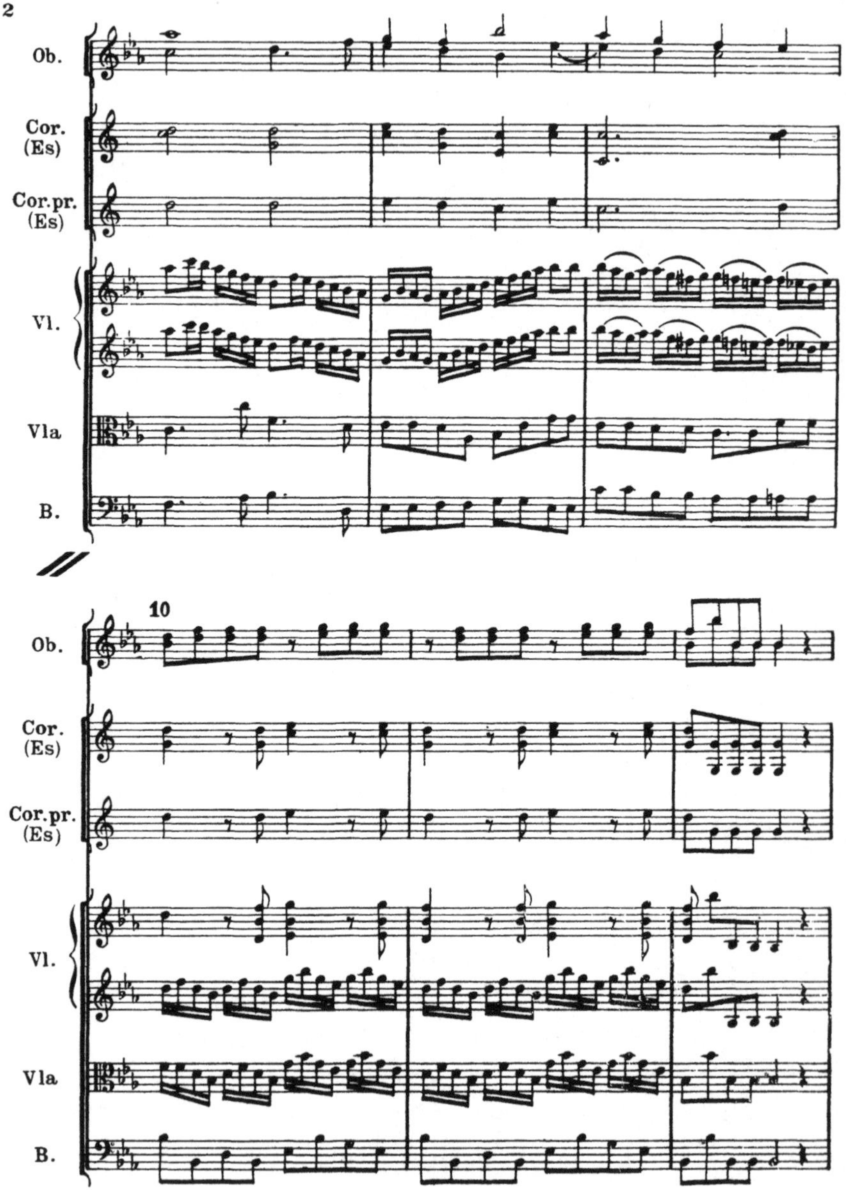
Ob.
Cor.
(Es)
Cor.pr.
(Es)
Vl.
Vla
B.
10
Ob.
Cor.
(Es)
Cor.pr.
(Es)
Vl.
Vla
B.

E. E. 6019

E.E.6019

10

E.E.6019

12

E.E.6019

14

E.E. 6019

E.E.6019

20

24

E.E.6019

II.

ROMANZA

E.E.6019

31

E.E.6019

32

III.

RONDO

Allegro vivace

34

36

38

E.E.6049

42

E.E. 6019

E.E.6019

46

E.E.6019

48

E.E.6019